Chickens, Hawks and Grumpy Goats

Five Years on a Farm

S.A. Molteni

ISBN-13: 978-1506137001
ISBN-10: 1506137008

Photographs by
S.A. Molteni

Cover by Pen Help
https://penhelp.wordpress.com

DEDICATION

Dedicated to all of the animals that have called our hobby farm their home. Some stayed a long while and some left way too soon.

CONTENTS

If having a soul means being able to feel love and loyalty and gratitude, then animals are better off than a lot of humans.

James Herriot, *All Creatures Great and Small*

Surviving the Winter

Winter is still in full swing and the coldness only makes our family more hungry. With too many mouths to feed and not enough nourishment, every day is a struggle to survive.

As the matriarch, I work in the morning to get the resources needed for the family to have at least one meal each day and I am not above killing the neighbors' chickens if I have to. Today, I have to. I am not proud of this fact, but it keeps the family going, at least for a few more days.

With three hungry offspring and a partner that works the overnight shift, it is up to me to keep them all fed during the day. When you have triplets to care for, every day brings with it a new dilemma. On the edge of starvation and not one friend in the neighborhood to offer me any help.

Do I feed the healthiest and strongest ones or the weakest and sickest one? No mother should have to choose.

The cold days wear on.

Well into January now and we lost one of the triplets. One of us had not gotten the needed nourishment to feed everyone and the youngest perished on the coldest night so far this winter.

Maybe it is no one's fault, but divine intervention to end the suffering of the sickly one.

With fewer mouths to feed, maybe we will make it through this god-forsaken, bitterly cold winter. If both of us, as parents, can keep the young ones fed and warm.

My partner thought it best to kill and steal another chicken from the neighbors' farm. If we only take one every couple of weeks, surely the farmer would not notice too much. Only a few more weeks and the little ones will be strong enough to fend for themselves.

Day and night, we work together to keep the little ones

warm and fed. There have been nights when predators wreaked havoc on our home and traumatized our offspring, but we fought for our lives and won the battles so far.

Into February, there are only a few more weeks until spring.

We are weak, giving the little ones most of the food we have. They are the most important thing right now. We have lived our lives and need the next generation to carry on for us. If we make it the next few weeks, we can thank the universe for seeing us through one more harsh winter.

We decide to chance it once more and go to the neighbors' farm for a much needed meal of chicken. We wait patiently for the most opportune time to go, just after dawn, right when the chickens are let out of their coop.

It is easier when the careless chickens do not keep a vigilant eye to the sky, but are focused on the morning feed and sparse amount of insects on the ground. We make our move. One stealthy swoop down from the old oak tree and the chicken's neck is broken - quick and painless.

We try to carry the carcass away, but in our weakened state we are too exhausted to move the small body.

The farmer sees us and charges out of his house with a shotgun. The farmer's wife is behind him. She is crying. It was her favorite chicken that we just killed. The death of her pet must be avenged.

Can't they see we are hungry, weak and mean them no harm?

The farmer aims, fires and does not miss.

My mate lost his life today, but the hawk chicks and I were spared to live another day on the edge of existence until the new spring comes.

Chicken Little in Therapy

It really wasn't her fault that the other fowl were killed by Foxy Loxy on that dreadful day so many years ago. But, that did not stop Chicken Little from blaming herself for their deaths. She had a classic case of survivor's guilt. If I had only not let my worry and anxiety get the better of me that day, my friends would still be here with me, she thought.

Preoccupied with her own regrets, Chicken Little did not see that the previous patient had left the office and that she was the only one remaining before office hours were over.

"Ms. Little, the doctor will see you now," the nurse announced.

As Chicken Little walked into the office, she was amazed at all of the diplomas, certificates and other awards that the doctor had nicely framed on the wall above his desk.

This guy must be a really good doctor - with all of these wonderful awards, she thought.

"Ms. Little, what brings you to see me today?" Dr. Drake asked as he turned around in his black leather, executive desk chair to greet the flustered hen.

"Mr. Drake, I have come to talk about this terrible guilt I have over the death of my friends," she responded.

"Please have a seat and let us begin," Dr. Drake continued.

As Chicken Little sat down on the couch, Dr. Drake began to ask questions about her life since the death of her friends and how she had coped up until this point with the stress of knowing that she was the sole survivor of the mass murder. Chicken Little could only respond that life had been stressful since then and she was barely coping.

The subsequent trial, conviction and execution of Foxy Loxy had brought back all of the bad memories she had of that horrible day and she continued to have nightmares every evening since the massacre. She was scared to walk in the woods, afraid that she might get hit on the head with another acorn, and terrified that she would encounter another fox that would try to kill her. The thought of the sky falling seemed to be ludicrous at present and the least of her worries.

She not only lived with the guilt of being the only one to escape, but lived in a constant state of fear and anxiety, worrying about the 'what ifs' and 'could have beens'. Her issues were too much for her rooster husband to bear and he subsequently flew the coop a few months ago.

"Ms. Little? Ms. Little? Hello, are you there?" Dr. Drake asked.

"Um, yes, sorry, I get lost in my thoughts sometimes," she replied.

"Ms. Little, it is quite common for you to feel the emotions you are feeling after such a traumatic experience and to recount it all on the witness stand. It will take time to work out the issues and heal from the wounds caused by the loss of your friends and the failure of your marriage," Dr. Drake continued.

"I am frightened that I will never be whole or be able to enjoy life again," Chicken Little responded.

"As a mental health professional, I assure you that your case can have a successful end. I have seen many that have been worse off and with missing limbs from similar attacks. You are very fortunate that you have no physical damage from your encounter."

"I do consider myself lucky in that regard," Chicken Little responded as she straightened her apron in her lap.

"Our hour is almost up. Is there anything further you want to discuss in this session?" Dr. Drake asked.

"No. Thanks for seeing me today."

As Chicken Little concluded her first meeting with Dr. Drake, she felt hopeful for the first time in a very long time. She had taken the first step in the journey to addressing her lifelong issues with panic, worry and anxiety.

A few days after her initial visit with Dr. Drake, Chicken Little noticed that she was not worrying so much and her fears seemed more controllable. She was even thinking about the future and possibly getting married again. Things she had not thought about since before the attack.

Thinking back on the first visit with Dr. Drake, she recalled that part of the time during the hour session, she did not remember some of what occurred. She only recollected being lost in her thoughts and finally coming back to reality halfway through the meeting. She wondered if she had been hypnotized, although she could not pinpoint when during the session that Dr. Drake could have put her under hypnosis.

During the next session, Chicken Little was the one to ask questions of Dr. Drake.

"Good afternoon, Ms. Little. How are you feeling today?" Dr. Drake asked.

"Actually, I am feeling much better than I did last week," she replied.

"That is great news, Ms. Little. Do you have anything you would like to discuss before we dive into this next session?" Dr. Drake asked.

"Actually, I do have a question, but I do not want to offend you with it. I need to know if you hypnotized me last week?" Chicken Little asked.

"Ms. Little, you were not exactly hypnotized. I merely 'suggested' things to you during our discussion last week to help you with the negative feelings your were experiencing. It is a method accepted by the medical community and patients all over the world." Dr. Drake explained.

"So, I was not placed under your control and instructed to 'act like a chicken'?" Chicken Little snidely asked.

"Well, you are a chicken, Ms. Little and I merely suggested that you act like one," Dr. Drake responded.

"So, that's it? You suggested that I act like a chicken and now I am cured?" Chicken Little demanded.

"My dear, you are feeling better, correct? You are less

worried, less anxious and less guilt-ridden, correct?" Dr. Drake responded.

"Well, yes, but I would rather not be subject to some 'quack' making suggestions on how I should act or allowing this same 'quack' to control my mind. That is unacceptable and I do not remember signing anything allowing you to do that," Chicken Little angrily responded.

"Ms. Little, the forms you filled out before our first appointment clearly stated that you would allow me, as your doctor, to do whatever was necessary to help you through your current crisis. This included hypnosis and if needed, confinement to a mental hospital," Dr. Drake calmly responded.

"Okay, granted, I filled out the paperwork. But, really, who reads every single word on those things?" Chicken Little jokingly asked.

"You are feeling much better than you were last week, Ms. Little. I can see a shimmer of light in your eyes that

was not there before. We will get through this together,"
Dr. Drake stated.

Half of the session was over before Chicken Little
realized that the conversation with Dr. Drake was helpful
and maybe she did need to 'act like a chicken' and stop
worrying so much about everything. Maybe this would
work after all, she thought.

The next session was more fruitful and Chicken Little
started to look forward to them with hope and with
happiness. Dr. Drake was handsome and he definitely
knew what he was doing, so Chicken Little listened
intently to everything he had to say in each of their
sessions over many months.

After a year of being counseled by Dr. Drake, Chicken
Little slowly began to enjoy life and move past the
negative things that were weighing her down. She even
went back to college and majored in psychology,
graduating at the top of her class. After a few years of
therapy, Chicken Little eventually became a partner in

the medical practice of Drake and Little and now goes by

the name of Chicken Little – Drake.

Sweet Pea, the Goat with an Attitude

Sweet Pea was the name given to the young nanny goat that we rescued from a bad situation of neglect and mistreatment.

We were not sure if she would make it through the night when she arrived at our hobby farm. We hoped for the best and did what we could to let her know she was loved and cared for. She made it through that first night and flourished as the days went by.

She liked apples, lettuce, carrots and just about any fruit or vegetable you would give her - as long as it was hand-fed to her. Once the food hit the ground, she was no longer interested in it and would turn her nose up at it. This was comical at first, but as time went on, this and other bad habits she had could not be overlooked.

We had never had goats before and thought that

rescuing one was a good thing. In hindsight, Sweet Pea should have been placed with a herd of goats, so as not to become a victim of the "lonely goat syndrome".

Our next door neighbor had two goats and we tried to introduce Sweet Pea to them, but she would have nothing to do with them. Her bleats of dissatisfaction rang out throughout the neighborhood during the two days she was near the other goats.

After her failure to socialize, we kept her in a side pasture away from our small herd of Black Angus cattle so that she could get healthy and focus on being a goat. After a few weeks, she regained her strength and became a bossy little handful of horned stubbornness.

During this time, she would constantly get her horns stuck in the fence, which we thought was an occasional mishap. But, later found it to be an everyday occurrence - actually multiple times a day.

On the advice of our veterinarian, we taped a hollow PVC pipe to her horns so that she could no longer push them through the wire fence material. This worked for a while until the tape fell off of the pipe and it detached from her horns. Then we would catch her with her head stuck in the fence again and have to wrangle her loose and tape the pipe back to her horns.

Once we were sure she was healthy, we decided to let her into the main pasture with the cows to see if she could get along with them. She loved being part of the herd and seemed happy to mingle with the cattle we had at the time. We felt we had done a great thing in rescuing her and giving her a home. Over time, this good feeling fell to the wayside.

In just a few days in the pasture with the cattle, Sweet Pea began ramming the cows with her horns every chance she could. Although she did not hurt the cows, it was an annoyance to them, especially during feeding time. We then had to feed Sweet Pea separately from the herd of cattle. It did not take us too long to realize that she was a goat with an attitude!

After a few months, we thought things had settled down to a good routine with Sweet Pea, so we took a trip out of town for a few days. It was then that we received a call from our neighbor who was taking care of the farm in our absence. Sweet Pea had gotten out of the pasture and could not be found. The next day, Sweet Pea was back in the pasture with the cows. A few days later, she disappeared again.

Once we came back from our trip, we searched and searched for her to no avail. There was no sign of her anywhere. That is until after about a week of us being back home.

We were leaving the farm to run into town for groceries and heard a distinct bleating sound coming from the roadway near our home. As we peeked around the corner from our driveway, we saw several goats running towards us down the dirt road that leads to our home. The leader of this gang of goats appeared to be Sweet Pea.

Once she saw us in the road, she immediately stopped in

her tracks, turned and ran the other way. We finally caught up with her and her posse at a farm that was several miles down another dirt road a few miles from our farm. This appeared to be Sweet Pea's new home.

It was apparent that Sweet Pea was not very happy when we left on vacation and decided that she was going to run away. She must have heard the bleats of the goats down the road and broke out of the pasture to get to them. She may have had second thoughts after making her escape and came back to our farm just to be sure that she truly wanted to leave us. But, in the end, she decided that being with a herd of her own kind and of her own choosing was where she wanted to be.

From our discussions with him, the owner of the herd of goats that Sweet Pea joined was happy to take her in as she was an intact female goat that could extend his herd in the future.

From time to time we see Sweet Pea leading the other goats around the pasture down the road. She has found her place in the world and we could not be happier for her.

The Best Christmas Eve Ever

As I wandered through the back pasture, checking the fences to make certain the storm that had just passed through did not down a tree on the barbed wire, I happened upon a turtle. This little guy was stuck in the lower part of the fence opening. When the heavy rains had come earlier in the day, he apparently tried to swim through the hole, but became immobilized when his shell lodged in the narrow opening.

He had been there awhile, noting from the scrapes on his leathery shell. He was exhausted and had all but given up on trying to escape the predicament that he was in. From his point of view, there was no way out except a slow agonizing death. Until a pair of human hands intervened and unwedged his body from the jaws of the heartless cattle fence.

He looked back as he swam away from me, acknowledging with a couple splashes in the water that surely said, "Thank you, whoever you are, for saving my life."

I smiled with a grateful heart and continued my walk as I had over two miles of fence to inspect before feeding time would again be upon me.

Near the halfway point of my stroll, I noticed an egret fishing in the pond that was overflowing with new rainwater. He was large, white and beautiful. When I approached just a little too close for his comfort, he spread his enormous bisque colored wings and flew gracefully over my head. He let out a call that felt like a song of gratitude as if to say, "Thanks for the great fishing today."

At the end of the journey around the property, I was relieved that I would not have to repair damaged fence and that there were no more animals in distress in the "back ten". After all, it was Christmas Eve and I wanted to finish the farm chores a little earlier than normal.

As I trotted into the barn with rubber boots caked with mud, the cows, pigs, chickens, ducks and turkeys chattered amongst themselves in anticipation of their evening meal. Excitement filled the air as I readied each dish with a special Christmas Eve treat for each of my furry or feathered friends.

The pigs received the remnants of freshly baked banana bread along with kale and other vegetables. The chickens received the seeds from several mild green peppers along with their normal cracked corn and layer crumbles. The ducks and turkeys were in heaven when they found their buckets filled with bits of bread - a rare and special treat for them along with their normal fowl feed.

Once the smaller creatures were taken care of, I focused my attention on the now two month old calves that I had been bottle-feeding since they were a few days old. The routine was to bring each of the two into separate large stalls in the quite roomy barn that is in the front part of the pasture. Each one went into their designated stall, where they ravenously finished drinking their dinner bottles and nibbled on the calf starter feed I had prepared. Their special treat this eve was an extra few minutes of brushing their beautifully soft coats.

Once the calves were finished eating their feed, I moved them into one single stall for the night where they groomed one another and lay down for the evening. I watched them laying in their mangers and my heart filled with joy to see them starting to doze off.

I quietly opened the stall door and gingerly tip-toed near them. The largest one, Latte was almost asleep when I sat next to her in her hay bed. I stroked her head and scratched her chin; she in return laid her head in my lap, wanting more pets and scratches. I could only continue as she nudged my hands to do so.

As I was sitting there with her head resting gently in my lap, my husband came into the stall and sat down beside me. The other baby calf, Chai, was almost asleep as well, so my husband began petting her head. Chai became very relaxed and slowly closed her eyes. With her head on the hay, eyes closed and her breathing almost the same sound of a kitten's purr, she stretched nearer to my husband.

We sat in the manger with our two baby cows for a good fifteen minutes, all the while with Latte's head using my leg as a pillow and Chai snoring to the continuous pets she was receiving from my husband. I looked at my husband and smiled. Then he sweetly and quietly said, "This is the best Christmas Eve ever."

I could only nod in agreement as I gently held my sleeping calf's head on my lap and did not want to move. Ultimately, I did not want a moment of this "best Christmas Eve ever" to end.

The Story Behind the Stories

In the winter of 2010, my father unexpectedly passed away. My husband and I lived in Seattle at the time and my parents lived in Florida.

After my father's funeral and after a leave of absence from work, my husband and I moved to Florida. His parents already lived in a retirement community there and my now widowed mother lived alone in the same area of the state.

Once a parent dies, you take inventory of your own life and try to pick out the things that are most important to you. I came to the conclusion that living so far from my family was not what I wanted to continue doing, so we devised a plan to move.

My husband and I had always talked about having some acreage and farm animals, but that was always some distant future plan and not something we could afford to do in Seattle. But, fate intervened and we found a fifteen acre farm with a "fixer-upper" farm house on it that was in foreclosure. We bid on the property and very quickly afterwards became the proud owners of a hobby farm.

* * *

The stories in this book are based on things that have happened on our farm over the past five years.

Surviving the Winter was a very hard story to write, in that my favorite chicken, Peepers, was ultimately killed by the family of hawks that lives near our home.

Peepers was a special pet and the emotional attachment I had to her was very strong. When she died, I wanted the hawk that killed her to also die. But, that would not bring Peepers back. So, I did the next best thing and wrote a story where the hawk lost his life. It helped me grieve the loss and move on to enjoying the sight of hawks again.

The next story, *Chicken Little in Therapy*, was created during the same period of time when our cochin bantam chickens were getting attacked on a regular basis by the same family of hawks.

One chicken, Dottie, survived the attack and I wanted to write a story from her perspective, only with a fox as the predator. In the end, the story became a mash-up of the children's story, *Chicken Little* and Dottie's view of the massacre – if chickens could talk ...

Sweet Pea, the Goat with an Attitude was a fun story to write, since it was a very funny episode in our hobby farm endeavor - when we tried our hand at caring for a rescue animal. Sweet Pea was a very strong-willed goat and made no attempt to hide the fact that she was stubborn with a knack for escaping any fenced in area.

My favorite story in this collection is *The Best Christmas Eve Ever*. In the fall of 2014, my husband and I decided to get two baby Jersey calves. They were days old when we adopted them and we had to bottle feed them three times a day for the first two months of their life.

On Christmas Eve, after all of the other farm animals were taken care of, we had some quiet time with the calves after their nightly bottle feeding. The story of what happened on Christmas Eve in a manger on a hobby farm in Florida was something that I will cherish forever.

* * *

The following is a stand-alone short story, *Her Name was Half Calf*, that was published on Amazon in January 2014. It also won an award on the website – *Midlife Collage*.

I have included it here as a bonus feature to this anthology, as it was the first story that I wrote about the farm. It is a very sad story about the death of a pet cow, in graphic detail in some sections. Please do not read it if this subject matter might offend you.

Her Name was Half Calf

She was a small black Angus heifer, born of Angus Girl who was the first cow we raised from a calf on our small hobby farm in northern Florida.

When Half Calf was a few weeks old, she became very sick, and we thought we would lose her. She had an intense stomach ailment and could not digest food or milk for several days. Thankfully, she made it through the illness and grew into a beautiful, ebony-colored cow with a touch of blonde on the tip of her tail. We grew very attached to her and for all intents and purposes, she was a pet.

When she was of breeding age, the neighbor's bull broke down the fence that separated the adjoining farm and introduced himself to Half Calf. Patching the fence and moving the cows could not keep the neighbor's bull away.

Ultimately, after many interludes and repaired fence lines, the owner relocated the bull elsewhere.

Many months went by and we were not sure if Half Calf was pregnant. Then her udder swelled, and she started to eat more than she normally did in the past. We calculated that she was about six months into the gestation period, and she would be calving in the coldest part of winter -- if we were correct.

We kept a close eye on Half Calf, looking for any sign that birth was imminent. Normally, when a cow is close to going into labor, a string of mucous is visible from the birth canal. There was no sign, and we began to think she was not pregnant after all.

We kept her in the front pasture with her mother, sister and their calves. She seemed restless and uncomfortable, but nothing out of the ordinary for a soon-to-be first-time mother.

When the weather dropped below freezing for several days, the cows and calves were not bothered by it and huddled together in the hay under an awning near the barn. The first night of freezing temperatures, we checked the cows until midnight and decided there was no indication that a calf was going to come. So we went to sleep.

We awoke early the next morning to find Half Calf on the ground in hard labor with her newborn halfway out of her birth canal. She was in extreme pain from trying to deliver her calf and was thoroughly exhausted when we found her.

We gathered the needed supplies to assist her in delivering: a chain to wrap around the baby, a winch for leverage, blankets, a heat lamp and warm water. With the help of a neighbor, my husband delivered the calf after wrapping a chain under the newborn's front hooves and pulling with the winch. But the baby bull was not breathing when he landed on the frozen ground. My husband gave him mouth to mouth and chest compressions. Amazingly, the baby bull started to breathe on his own. So we covered him in a blanket and placed a heat lamp near him for warmth.

By this time, Half Calf should have been on her feet waiting for her newborn to start nursing. She lay on the ground, however, unable to stand. We coaxed and prodded her without success. We knew something else must be wrong, so we called the large animal veterinarian to make a house call.

The vet came within an hour but the calf had died, and we knew Half Calf was not well. The vet determined Half Calf might have internal bleeding and gave her an intravenous concoction of various medicines along with a vitamin and electrolyte mixture that was administered to her via a feeding tube.

The vet advised that we watch Half Calf and let her rest. Once she rested for a few hours, we were to roll her from side to side and continue to coax her to her feet. We were warned that the longer she stayed on the ground, the less likely it would be that she would recover.

For the next day and a half, we rolled Half Calf from side to side every four hours. We made sure she was comfortable, fed and had water. She looked as though she was recovering on the second day and had some energy to attempt to lift herself. On the third day, however, we found her breathing heavily and holding her head in a strange angle on a hay bale. She was uninterested in food or water and appeared depressed.

From that point, she seemed to lose her will to live. She would not cooperate with us when we rolled her. She would move back into the position from which we moved her. She refused to eat or drink and made low moaning sounds when we approached her. The vet surmised her lungs were most likely filling with fluid, and she would eventually suffocate if she continued to stay immobile.

We tried several more times to get her to her feet. On the last attempt, she screamed the most haunting, blood-curdling moo that we had ever heard come from a cow. It was her way of saying, "Stop. I am done. No more."

We had never been in this position before, having to be the voice for an animal that had lost her will to live. We wanted to do everything we could to give her a chance to recover, but we did not want her to suffer a long painful death by drowning in her own fluids. It also became apparent to us that Half Calf was paralyzed on one side of her hindquarters. We knew that euthanasia was the only answer.

We decided that if Half Calf was going to die, we wanted her carcass used for something positive. We located a company that would come to our farm and take Half Calf to be processed into food for a local big cat sanctuary. At least her death would give life to abused and abandoned lions, tigers and leopards.

A man from the company came late in the afternoon on the third day. We had already said our goodbyes to Half Calf and thought that the man would take her alive to the processing plant. But the man who came to our farm told us that he would have to euthanize her on-site.

My husband and I agreed that he would be the one present when she died, and I would stay in the house until after Half Calf was loaded onto to the truck. Because I'm squeamish, I thought that was a good plan for everyone involved. But in the back of my mind, I knew that I needed to see what happened when an animal was "put down."

When the moment came for Half Calf to take her last breath, I looked out the window as the man raised his gun to the space between Half Calf's eyes. I covered my ears and stared as my husband stood near the man who would kill my favorite cow. Through a fountain of tears, I witnessed her life being taken from me.

For many months after her death, I would tell myself daily that we made the right decision for Half Calf. This reassurance has not lessened the emotional impact her death has had on me.

Death is ugly. I still cry. I still miss her.

ABOUT THE AUTHOR

After over 30 years in the IT industry, S.A. Molteni is a retired systems engineer. She is also currently a hobby farmer, avid traveler and an author of several award-winning short stories. She lives on a small homestead with her husband and a menagerie of farm animals.

S.A. Molteni can be found on the following social media sites:

Blog - http://samolteni.blogspot.com/
Facebook - https://www.facebook.com/author.samolteni
Twitter - https://twitter.com/samolteni

43709040R00028

Made in the USA
Middletown, DE
27 April 2019